My First Pet

Turtles

by Cari Meister

Bullfrog
Books

Ideas for Parents and Teachers

Bullfrog Books let children practice reading informational text at the earliest reading levels. Repetition, familiar words, and photo labels support early readers.

Before Reading

- Ask the child to think about turtles. Ask: What do you know about turtles?

- Look at the picture glossary together. Read and discuss the words.

Read the Book

- "Walk" through the book and look at the photos. Let the child ask questions. Point out the photo labels.

- Read the book to the child, or have him or her read independently.

After Reading

- Prompt the child to think more. Ask: What do you need to take care of a turtle? Would you like to own one as a pet?

Bullfrog Books are published by Jump!
5357 Penn Avenue South
Minneapolis, MN 55419
www.jumplibrary.com

Library of Congress Cataloging-in-Publication Data

Meister, Cari, author.
  Turtles / by Cari Meister.
      pages cm. — (My first pet)
  Summary: "This photo-illustrated book for early readers tells how to take care of a pet turtle" — Provided by publisher.
  Audience: Ages 5-8.
  Audience: K to grade 3.
  Includes bibliographical references and index.
  ISBN 978-1-62031-126-4 (hardcover) —
  ISBN 978-1-62496-193-9 (ebook) —
  ISBN 978-1-62031-148-6 (paperback)
  1. Turtles as pets — Juvenile literature. 2. Turtles — Juvenile literature. I. Title.
  SF459.T8M45 2015
  639.3'92—dc23

2013049160

Series Editor: Rebecca Glaser
Series Designer: Ellen Huber
Book Designer: Anna Peterson
Photo Researcher: Casie Cook

Photo Credits: Alamy/Arco Images GmbH, 10–11; Corbis/Margot Hartford/First Light, 9; Shutterstock/hsagencia, 22 (worm); Shutterstock/motorolka, 22 (lettuce); Shutterstock/topseller, 22 (strawberry); Dreamstime.com/Tonny Anwar, 14–15; Dreamstime.com/Carleato, 18 (inset), 23bl; Shutterstock/Dusit, 22 (heat lamp); Shutterstock/Alias Studiot Oy, 22 (tank); Shutterstock/Anneka, 3; Shutterstock/Bojan Pipalovic, 24; Shutterstock/Chantal de Bruijne, 5; Shutterstock/dora modly-paris, 16, 23tl; Shutterstock/Eric Isselee, 8; Shutterstock/IrinaK, 1, 17; Shutterstock/kohy, 6–7; Shutterstock/Mila Supinskaya, 23br; Shutterstock/Olga Popova, 22 (turtle); SuperStock, cover; SuperStock/Blend Images, 20–21; SuperStock/FLPA, 12–13, 23tr; SuperStock/Gerard Lacz Images, 4; SuperStock/Minden Pictures, 18–19

Printed in the United States of America at Corporate Graphics, in North Mankato, Minnesota.
3-2014
10 9 8 7 6 5 4 3 2 1

Table of Contents

A New Pet

Kim wants a turtle.

She goes to a shelter.
Many turtles there
need homes.

A turtle can live
a long time.

Many people get one.

But they get tired
of caring for it.

Kim picks Tex.

She will take good care of him.

A turtle needs
a big tank.

It can get sick
if it does not
have room.

heat
lamp

A turtle is cold-blooded.
It needs a heat lamp.
Then it can keep warm.

Turtles like water.
They need a place
to swim.

A turtle needs food.
Jay has a box turtle.

He feeds her worms.
Yum!

Turtles like mud.

They have sharp claws.

They dig.

They cover up with mud.

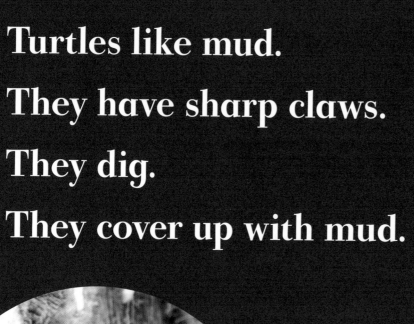

claw

Turtles are cool pets!

What Does a Turtle Need?

tank
Make sure your tank is large enough for your turtle.

heat lamp
Turtles need a heat lamp in their tanks to keep warm.

food
Turtles can eat many foods, such as worms, insects, vegetables, and fruits.

Picture Glossary

box turtle
A small turtle that can close its shell all the way when it pulls in its head and legs.

cold-blooded
When an animal's body temperature changes with the air around it.

claw
A hard nail on the foot of an animal.

shelter
A place where people take care of animals that do not have homes.

Index

To Learn More

Learning more is as easy as 1, 2, 3.

1) Go to www.factsurfer.com

2) Enter "pet turtle" into the search box.

3) Click the "Surf" button to see a list of websites.

With factsurfer.com, finding more information is just a click away.